Have You *Suffered* Enough?

Other Books by Bill Ferguson

How to Heal a Painful Relationship
And if Necessary, How to Part as Friends

Miracles are Guaranteed
A Step-by-Step Guide to Restoring Love, Being Free, And Creating A Life That Works

Audio Cassettes and CDs

How to Heal a Painful Relationship

Have You Suffered Enough?

How to Divorce as Friends

How to Love Yourself

How to Have Love in Your Life

How to be Free of Guilt and Resentment

How to be Free of Upset and Stress

How to Create a Life That Works

How to Create Prosperity

How to Find Your Purpose

How to Experience Your Spirituality

Spirituality: Teachings from a World Beyond

Have You *Suffered* Enough?

BILL FERGUSON

Return to the Heart
P.O. Box 541813
Houston, TX 77254

www.billferguson.com
www.divorceasfriends.com
www.effectiveliving.com

HAVE YOU SUFFERED ENOUGH?

Return to the Heart
P.O. Box 541813
Houston, Texas 77254
U.S.A.
(713) 520-5370

Copyright © 2002 by Bill Ferguson

All rights reserved. No part of this book may be reproduced by any mechanical, photographic, or electronic process, or in the form of an audio recording, nor may it be stored in a retrieval system, transmitted, or otherwise be copied for public or private use without the written permission of the publisher.

Cover design by Mark Gelotte
Cover photo by Michael Hart

Library of Congress
Catalog Card Number: 2001-130829

First Edition

ISBN 1-878410-28-8

Printed in the United States of America

This book is dedicated to Sue: my wife, my partner and my best friend.

CONTENTS

1. YOU CAN BE FREE 1

2. THE NATURE OF UPSETS 8

3. THE EXPERIENCE OF LOVE 15

4. RESISTING SABOTAGES YOUR LIFE 22

5. HOW THE HURT BEGINS 29

6. MAKE PEACE WITH YOURSELF 36

7. JUDGMENT IS AN ILLUSION 43

8. TWO SIDES OF THE COIN 52

9. CREATE A NEW FREEDOM 58

10. RELEASE YOUR SUPPRESSED HURT 64

Contents

11. Start the Healing Process 72

12. Find Your Hurt 79

13. Face the Dragon 91

14. Steps For More Healing 99

15. Be Free of Guilt 107

16. Let go of Resentment 115

17. Make Peace with Your Parents 123

18. Allow Yourself to be Human 131

19. The Opportunity is Yours 141

Be free of the hidden core issues that destroy love and sabotage your life.

Have you ever noticed that there are certain areas of your life where you consistently suffer? Do the same self-sabotaging behavior patterns keep showing up in your life? Do you keep having the same type of upsets, over and over?

Ultimately, all of your suffering and all of your self-sabotaging behavior are the result of hidden core issues from your past. These issues are created by the automatic avoidance of a very specific hurt.

When these issues get triggered, they produce a state of fear and upset that destroys love and forces you to interact in a way that sabotages your life. Until you heal this hurt, you are guaranteed to repeat the past.

Finding and healing this hurt is one of the most important things you can ever do. This book will show you how.

Chapter 1

YOU CAN BE FREE

When you were a young child, you were pure love. You were happy, alive and free. This is the essence of who you are. This is your natural state.

Unfortunately, you were born into a world that suppresses this state. Instead of being born into a world that is loving and supportive, you were born into a world that is critical and harsh.

Before long, you experienced invalidation, rejection and painful losses of love. You felt this hurt from your parents, your friends and the world around you.

As a little child, the only way you could explain this loss of love was to blame yourself.

In a moment of hurt, you decided that you were

worthless, not good enough, not worth loving, a failure, or in some other way, *not okay*.

This wasn't the truth, but in the eyes of a child, this became your truth. This was the only explanation that made any sense at the time.

You then hated the very notion that you created. "No one can ever love me if I'm worthless. Worthless is a horrible way to be."

The moment you bought the notion that you were *not okay*, you created an internal mechanism, or core issue, that would then sabotage the rest of your life. From that moment on, the underlying focus of your life would be to avoid this hurt.

A good way to see this hurt is to notice what happens the moment you get upset. Notice the immediate and powerful surge of feelings and emotion that comes forth. This is the hurt that runs your life.

You may never notice this hurt, but it is certainly there. It determines your actions and shapes your life.

The automatic avoidance of this hurt also forces you to interact in a way that creates all sorts of suffering.

Whenever something comes along that reactivates this hurt, you feel threatened. In an instinctive attempt to avoid this hurt, you fight and resist.

This automatic fighting and resisting then creates a state of fear and upset that destroys your effectiveness and almost always makes your situation worse.

You get upset and close down inside. You lose your creativity and your ability to see clearly. You get tunnel vision. All you can do is fight, resist, hang on or withdraw.

This state of resisting then destroys love and creates opposition and resistance against yourself. Instead of having your life work, you make your life more difficult.

Without knowing, you interact in a way that actually creates more of the very hurt that you are avoiding.

Here is an example that illustrates this:

When Rhonda was growing up, her father was so occupied with his work that he seldom paid any attention to her. When he did pay attention, he would yell at her. She felt totally unloved.

As a result, Rhonda couldn't help but adopt the belief that she wasn't worth loving. This wasn't the truth, but this became a hurt that she would run from for the rest of her life.

To avoid this hurt, Rhonda would interact in a way that would sabotage all of her relationships.

She was so afraid of being alone and feeling her hurt, that she never had the patience to find the person who was right for her. She would settle for anyone who was half-way acceptable. As a result, none of her relationships worked.

Even if she found the perfect person, she would get upset over and over because the other person wouldn't treat her a certain way or wouldn't give her enough love and attention.

She would also hang on to the person. She would hang on because, if the person left, she would have to face even more hurt. Her hanging on would then push the person even further away.

Eventually, all the men in her life would leave. Rhonda did everything she could to be worth loving, but everything she did to avoid her hurt created more of it.

The same thing happens to every one of us. The specifics are different, but the process is the same.

Every one of us has a hurt that runs our life. For one person, this is the hurt of feeling inadequate or not worth loving. For another, it's the hurt of feeling not good enough, worthless or some other form of *not okay*.

It's the subconscious avoidance of this hurt that creates the suffering in our lives. Every aspect of your life that doesn't work can be traced to this hurt.

The avoidance of this hurt is responsible for virtually all your fear and all your upsets. It is responsible for all your conflict and all your self-sabotaging behavior.

To be free inside and to be effective in life, you need to discover what your hurt is and be free of it. This is probably the single, most important thing you can ever do.

Once you heal this hurt, your whole life begins to change.

Instead of creating a life of fear and upset, you create a life of love. You restore the happiness, the freedom and the aliveness that you once had. You see life clearly and you become far more effective.

You can then create a life that works for you instead of against you.

The process of finding and healing your hurt is very simple and very fast. This book will show you how. All you need is the desire to be free.

ACTION TO TAKE

1. Make a list of the areas of your life that don't work. Where do you suffer?

2. Any area of your life that doesn't work will be an area where you feel threatened. To avoid this threat, you automatically fight and resist. Notice the fear and upset that exists in these areas of life.

3. See if you can find the hurt that is under your fear and upset. What do these areas of life imply or suggest about you? Do they say that you are worthless, not good enough, not worth loving or a failure?

4. Now recall the hurt that you experienced as a child. Notice that this hurt is the same hurt that runs your life today.

5. Are you willing to be free of this hurt? Are you willing to create a life that works better than anything you ever dreamed possible? If you are, use this book to learn how. Make sure you do the various exercises.

Chapter 2

THE NATURE OF UPSETS

We all want to be happy, but we are convinced that happiness comes from outside of ourselves. We believe that happiness is determined by what we have and by what happens around us.

We then go through life trying to force life to be a certain way. We think that this will bring us the happiness that we seek, but it never does. In fact, the more we try to force life to make us happy, the more we create a life of fear and upset, and the more unhappy we become.

Happiness can never come from anything outside of yourself. It can only come from within. This is because happiness is an inner state.

When you are full of joy, where is the joy located? Is the joy outside of you or is the joy inside?

Obviously, the joy is inside. When you are upset, where is your upset located? It's inside of you.

At any given moment, you are having certain body sensations, certain thoughts, feelings and emotions. These combine to give you a very particular experience of life.

Notice the particular experience of life that you are having right now. What body sensations are you having? What thoughts and feelings are you having?

It's the experience of life that you have at any moment that determines the quality of your life.

When you are full of love, joy and inner peace, the quality of your life is great. You feel good about yourself and good about life. You are confident, creative and very effective. Life works effortlessly.

When you are full of fear and upset, the quality of your life is not so great. You become negative and full of resistance. Life becomes difficult.

The particular experience you have at any given time seems to be a function of what happens around you, but it's not. Your happiness, or lack thereof, is a function of how you relate to what happens.

THE NATURE OF UPSETS

A good way to see this is to look at the nature of upsets.

When we get upset, the upset seems to be caused by our circumstances, but this is an illusion. Upsets are not caused by our circumstances. Upsets are caused by fighting and resisting our circumstances.

To see this in your life, select a recent upset. Now go to the moment the upset began. Didn't something happen? Didn't that circumstance happen whether you liked it or not? Of course. No matter how upset you got, that event still happened.

Now notice what would happen to the upset if, by some miracle, you were totally at peace with what happened. There would be no upset.

There would be no upset because the upset wasn't caused by what happened. The upset was caused by fighting and resisting what happened.

If you could somehow remove the fighting and resisting, the upset would disappear. You would restore both your effectiveness and your peace of mind.

This is the key to having life work.

When you are free of fear and upset, you are creative, resourceful and able to discover solutions. You see your situation clearly and you know what needs to be done.

When you fight a particular aspect of life, you create a state of fear and upset. You get tunnel vision. You then interact in a way that destroys love and creates a state of opposition and resistance against yourself.

If you want your life to work, you need to be free of the fear and upset. You need to be able to flow with life.

Unfortunately, this is much easier said than done. Flowing with life is often very difficult. This is because the circumstances of life are forever reactivating your suppressed hurt.

The moment this happens, you feel threatened. In an instinctive attempt to avoid this hurt, you fight and resist. This in turn creates a state of fear and upset that sabotages your life.

The circumstances of life don't have the power to

THE NATURE OF UPSETS

create an upset inside of you. Circumstances can only strike a nerve that is already there.

This is why the same thing can happen to two different people, and one person will get upset and the other won't. Different people get upset at different things because each person has a different set of suppressed hurt.

Now notice that the same type of upset keeps showing up in your life. The same type of upset keeps showing up because the same hurt keeps getting reactivated.

We think that the quality of life is a function of what happens around us, but it's not. It's a function of our ability to flow with what happens.

As long as we believe that happiness and upsets are caused by our circumstances, we will continue to fight and resist. We will try to force life to be a certain way in a subconscious attempt to make us happy.

Unfortunately, this never works. Instead of creating the happiness that we seek, we push our happiness away.

If you want to have your life be as great as it can

be, learn how to flow with life. Instead of fighting and resisting your circumstances, put your focus on healing your hurt and creating a life that works.

THE NATURE OF UPSETS

ACTION TO TAKE

1. Make a list of your major upsets. Then, for each upset, notice what would happen if you were totally at peace with what happened. Notice that there would be no upset.

2. Now notice that the same type of upset keeps showing up in your life. The same type of upset keeps showing up because the same suppressed hurt keeps getting reactivated.

3. Upsets are not caused by what happens. Upsets are caused by your fighting and resisting what happens. Look at your upsets and see that this is true. Notice the hurt that's under each upset.

4. Notice what happens to your peace of mind when you get upset. What happens to your ability to see clearly? What happens to your effectiveness? Notice that getting upset only makes your situation worse.

Chapter 3

THE EXPERIENCE OF LOVE

The key to having life work is to create the experience of love. When the experience of love is present, you are confident, creative and full of energy. You are happy and alive. You feel good about yourself and good about life. Life is effortless and great things happen.

Ultimately, this is the happiness that we seek. This is what we want in our relationships and in our lives.

Look at the times in your life that you consider to have been the very best. These are the times when you lived in this state.

If you want your life to be as great as it can be, it's important to create the experience of love.

THE EXPERIENCE OF LOVE

So what creates the experience of love? Is it communication? Openness? Trust? All of these are valuable, but none of them create the experience of love.

You create the experience of love by giving acceptance and appreciation. You destroy it by resisting, by being non-accepting.

A good way to see this is to look at relationships.

Notice how you feel when someone genuinely accepts and appreciates you. Doesn't this feel great? Of course it does. You feel better about yourself and better about life. You also feel better about the person who accepts and appreciates you.

The same thing happens when you give acceptance and appreciation to someone else. That person feels better about him or herself, better about life, and better about you.

By giving acceptance and appreciation, you create the experience of love. You then receive acceptance and appreciation in return.

Any relationship, and any aspect of your life that

works great, will be an area where you are full of acceptance and appreciation.

You destroy love by resisting, by being non-accepting, judgmental and critical.

Notice how you feel when someone is non-accepting and critical toward you. Instantly, the experience of love disappears. You feel hurt and upset. You close down inside. You put up your walls of protection and you automatically resist the person who is non-accepting toward you.

The same thing happens when you are non-accepting toward someone else. That person gets upset, puts up his or her walls of protection and automatically becomes critical and resentful toward you.

By being non-accepting, you destroy the experience of love. You then receive non-acceptance in return.

Then it gets worse.

As the other person becomes critical and resentful of you, you get more upset. Your walls of protection get stronger and you become more critical of the other person. Then the other person gets more upset and becomes more resentful of you. Then you become more resentful toward the other person.

Without knowing, you create a cycle of conflict, a cycle of resisting, attacking and withdrawing from each other.

This cycle then goes on and on without either person noticing his or her role in the conflict. It destroys the experience of love and produces tremendous suffering.

If you have any relationship that isn't working, this cycle is present. Just look. You are resisting the way that person is. That person then gets upset and resists you in turn.

By resisting, you destroy the experience of love. You also create opposition and resistance against yourself. This is the nature of resistance. Whatever you resist gets worse.

Look at any area of your life that isn't working. This will be an area where you are resisting. If you could somehow let go of the resistance, that area of your life would clear up.

Unfortunately, this is much easier said than done. Some people and some aspects of life are very difficult to accept. Fortunately, resisting is just a state of mind, and it doesn't improve a thing.

Find someone in your life who is difficult to accept. Now take a good look at this person. Doesn't this person have a very particular view of life and a very particular way of behaving?

Now look a little further. Isn't this person exactly the way he or she is? Isn't this person this way without any regard for how you feel about it?

You can hate the way this person is, or you can love the way this person is. How you feel about the person is totally irrelevant. This person is still the way he or she is.

This is also true about your life. At any moment, your life is exactly the way it is. The people in your life are exactly the way they are, and you are the way you are.

Pick any aspect of your life that you don't like. Notice that this aspect of your life is exactly the way it is.

THE EXPERIENCE OF LOVE

Your demands and expectations for how life should be have nothing to do with the way life is. No matter how upset you get, your life is still the way that it is.

Acceptance is nothing more than surrendering to the truth.

When you are at peace with the truth, you remain free inside. You see your situation clearly, and you can see what needs to be done. You can then interact in a way that creates the experience of love and that has life work for you instead of against you.

When you fight the truth, you destroy the experience of love. You get upset and close down. You lose your ability to see clearly, and you interact in a way that creates opposition and resistance against yourself.

Resisting doesn't make your situation better. Resisting makes your situation worse.

Action To Take

1. At any moment, your life is exactly the way it is. The people in your life are the way they are, and you are the way you are. Look in your life and see that this is true. Notice how irrelevant your feelings are.

2. Notice what happens when you fight and resist the way life is. Notice the fear and upset that gets created. Notice that being upset only makes your situation worse.

3. Look at any relationship you have that isn't working. Notice that the other person is the way he or she is and that you are fighting it. Notice that by resisting this person, you destroy love and fuel the cycle of conflict.

4. Make a list of all the areas of your life where you resist. Notice the freedom you would have if you could flow with these areas of life. Notice how much more effective you would be.

Chapter 4

RESISTING SABOTAGES YOUR LIFE

Resisting is just a state of mind, but it's a state of mind that is guaranteed to sabotage your life. The moment you resist, you start a process that actually brings to you the very circumstances that you are trying to avoid.

For example, let's say that you are married and that you have a fear of losing your spouse. The more you resist losing your spouse, the more you hang on, and the more you push your spouse further and further away.

By resisting the loss of your spouse, you create a state of fear and upset that actually makes your fear come true.

Here's another example. Look at how you feel when someone tries to change you. How do you feel about changing? You don't want to. You get upset and become resistant. You don't want to change a thing.

The same thing happens when you resist someone else or any aspect of your life. The very act of resisting makes whatever you resist more solid.

Imagine four yellow balloons on the ceiling above you. Now don't think about them. Whatever you do, don't think about those large yellow balloons on the ceiling above you. You just thought about them. Don't do that. Stop.

Notice what happens when you resist the thought of the balloons. You keep thinking about them. In fact, you can hardly think about anything else. By resisting the thought of yellow balloons, you give the thought power and keep it alive.

Resisting is one of the most powerful ways that we create the circumstances of our lives. Whatever you resist gets stronger. It's a law of physics.

Resisting will also keep you from seeing what needs to be done.

Resisting keeps you from seeing the truth.

At any moment, your life is exactly the way that it is. This is true whether you like it or not. When you resist, you are resisting the truth.

When you fight the truth, you create a state of fear and upset that destroys your ability to see the truth. When you can't see the truth, you can't see the action that you need to take.

Here's an example that illustrates this:

Marci was unreliable and her husband Michael hated it. He needed to rely on her because they worked together. When she didn't do her part, he got upset. He did everything he could to change her, but nothing worked. Marci continued to be unreliable.

Finally, after years of relying on her and suffering the consequences, Michael had a realization that changed his life. He realized that Marci wasn't reliable.

This would have been obvious to anyone else, but Michael couldn't see it. He couldn't see the truth because he didn't want this to be the truth. He wanted Marci to be reliable.

Once he stopped resisting and let in the truth, he saw his situation clearly. He didn't like what he saw, but he could see what he needed to do. For starters, he needed to stop relying on her. He then handled his affairs accordingly.

As long as Michael resisted the truth, he was ineffective. All he could do was fight and resist, which in turn destroyed love and made his situation worse. The moment he stopped resisting, this area of his life began to clear up.

Any area of your life that isn't working is an area where you are resisting.

Take a moment and notice how true this is. Find any area of your life that isn't working and notice how much you are resisting it. Notice the fear and upset that surrounds this area.

Now notice the tunnel vision that's present.

Resisting creates tunnel vision.

Whenever you resist, you have tunnel vision. You have tunnel vision because, subconsciously, your circumstances are a threat to your survival.

All your energy and focus is then directed toward the removal of this threat. You are forced to fight, resist, hang on or withdraw. There are no other options in the tunnel vision.

Unfortunately, the tunnel vision is so narrow that it destroys your ability to discover what works. In fact, what works becomes irrelevant.

"Don't bother me with what works. I'm not interested. Show me how to remove the threat. I'm interested in that."

This narrow focus makes it very difficult to discover solutions.

For example, if you are resisting the loss of someone, you will automatically hang on, and the more you hang on, the more you will push the person away.

If you want the other person to stay, it helps to say something like this: "I give you your freedom. I let you go. I don't want you to go, but I want you to be happy. You have my blessings whatever you do, and I love you whether you go or stay. I hope you stay."

If you can say this and mean it, you will remove much of the other person's resistance toward you. The chance of the other person staying then increases substantially.

This is a great example of what works, but if you are in the tunnel vision, this would never be an option. "Let go of her? You're crazy. I'm not going to do that. Tell me how to make her stay."

Resisting creates a state of tunnel vision that destroys your ability to see what needs to be done. Instead of doing what works, you do what doesn't work.

So why do we resist? Why can't we flow with life? Why can't we be at peace with the truth?

We fight the truth because the truth triggers our suppressed hurt. It triggers the old hurt of feeling worthless, not good enough, not worth loving or some other form of feeling *not okay*.

In a subconscious attempt to avoid this hurt, we fight and resist.

To be free of the automatic resisting and to create a life that works, you need to find and heal this hurt.

Action To Take

1. Resisting is one of the most powerful ways that we create suffering in our lives. Notice that any area of your life that doesn't work is an area where you are resisting. If you could let go of the resistance, that area of life would clear up.

2. Resisting is a state of mind and is totally separate from your actions. By letting go of your resistance, you remove the fear and upset that destroys your ability to see what needs to be done. You also remove the resistance that you have created against yourself. Work with this concept until you see that this is true.

3. We resist in a subconscious attempt to avoid the suppressed hurt that our circumstances reactivate. We don't want to feel the hurt of feeling worthless, not good enough or some other form of *not okay*. What is the hurt that you are avoiding?

4. Notice the freedom that you would gain if you were free of the fear and upset that comes from resisting.

Chapter 5

How the Hurt Begins

Several years ago, I was shopping in a local department store when I saw a mother yelling at her little four-year-old daughter. Apparently the little girl spilled her soft drink, and the mother was quite embarrassed.

"What's the matter with you?" the mother yelled. "Why are you so stupid?"

The mother was so loud and hateful that everyone stopped and stared. The little girl was devastated. She experienced a very painful loss of love and started crying.

Then the little girl did something that would forever change her life. She bought the notion that she was stupid.

Clearly this wasn't the truth, but to the girl, this was the absolute truth. She was permanently, totally and hopelessly stupid. What else could she conclude?

"My mom knows everything, and she says I'm stupid. Clearly this must be true. Besides, I did spill my drink, and yesterday I got my shoes muddy."

The little girl couldn't help but buy the notion that she is stupid. This is especially true if her mother tells her this over and over.

Imagine how painful this must be. The girl started out being free and alive – full of love and joy. Then she discovered that something was terribly wrong with her. She was stupid. The hurt of this realization would have been unbearable.

Then the little girl took the process one step further. She started fighting the very notion that she created.

"No one can ever love someone who's stupid. Look at my mom. Even my mom doesn't love me because I'm stupid. Stupid is a horrible way to be. I can't be stupid. If I'm stupid, I might as well just die."

The little girl will then spend the rest of her life running from stupid trying desperately to become smart.

Then, if any circumstance comes along that hints that she really is stupid, that circumstance will be a serious threat to her survival. She will have to fight and resist it with all her might.

This in turn creates a state of fear and upset that destroys her ability to see clearly and quickly makes her situation worse.

She'll never notice, but by resisting the notion that she is stupid, stupid will become a major part of her life; and the more she resists it, the more it will show up in her life.

For example, have you ever known people who have to be right? These people are usually running from stupid. To prove they are smart, they have to make everyone else wrong.

The problem with this is that if you go around having to be right and making other people wrong, you alienate them. You force them to retaliate by showing you how wrong and stupid you are. By running from stupid, you create more stupid.

The same thing happens no matter what your hurt is.

If you are running from the hurt of feeling not worth loving, you will sabotage your relationships. You will get upset easily. You will hang on and do everything you can to force people to treat you in a certain way.

This in turn destroys the experience of love. It fuels the cycle of conflict and pushes people away. Everything you do to avoid the hurt of feeling not worth loving creates more of it.

If you are running from failure, you will tend to either take unrealistic chances in a desperate attempt to become a success, or you will be so afraid of failure that you won't be able to take a risk. Either way, you create more failure.

Whatever you avoid and resist, you will create.

Look in your life and see how true this is. Notice that whatever you avoid and resist keeps showing up in your life.

As long as you live, life will keep bringing you the very hurt that you are trying to get away from. Once you find and heal this hurt, you no longer need to run from it and life no longer needs to bring it to you.

The best way to find and heal this hurt is to look at your upsets. In fact, you could say that this is the purpose of upsets. Upsets are brought to you so that you can discover and heal the hurt that creates your suffering.

To find the hurt that runs your life, make a list of every major upset that you can think of. List all the times that you have been angry or hurt. Make the list as complete as you can.

Then look at the hurt that is under each upset. Find the words of *not okay* that most describe the hurt. For each upset, ask yourself the question, "What do those circumstances say about me?"

If someone leaves you and this is painful, this could say that you are not worth loving. If you get fired from a job, this could say that you are a failure.

Find the words of *not okay* that hurt the most. The more painful the words, the closer you are to the hurt.

Keep in mind, you are not looking for the truth,

you are looking for the hurt. The truth and the hurt have absolutely nothing to do with each other. They are totally separate.

To say that the little girl is stupid has nothing to do with the truth, but it has everything to do with her hurt.

Look for the hurt that is under your upsets. Then notice that the same hurt keeps showing up in your life. Find the words that most accurately describe this hurt.

We will work with this in more depth later, but for now, get a general idea of what your hurt is.

Would it be painful if you really were worthless and had no value? Would it be painful if you were not good enough, not worth loving or a failure?

What are the words that hurt the most? Keep looking.

Action To Take

1. Make a list of every major upset that you have had during your life. Make the list as complete as you can.

2. See if you can find the hurt that is under each upset. Find the words of *not okay* that most describe this hurt. For each upset, ask yourself the question, "What do those circumstances say about me?" Find the words that hurt the most.

3. Notice that the hurt and the truth have absolutely nothing to do with each other. Notice that the same hurt runs through all your upsets.

4. How would you feel if you really were worthless, not good enough or whatever your issue is? How would you feel if this were the absolute truth? Notice how painful this would be.

5. Get in touch with this hurt. Notice how threatening it is. Wouldn't you do almost anything to avoid feeling this hurt? Notice how much this hurt runs your life.

Chapter 6

MAKE PEACE WITH YOURSELF

After you discover the aspects of you that you are resisting, the next step is to make peace with them.

"But I don't want to make peace with them. I want to get rid of them."

Well, you can't. In fact, everything you do to get rid of them gives them more power. Remember the yellow balloons? The more you fight the yellow balloons, the more yellow balloons you get.

The same is true for any aspect of you that you are avoiding. If you are avoiding *worthless*, for example – and most people are – everything you do to get rid of *worthless* gives it more power.

To be free of the hurt of *worthless*, or any other

aspect, you need to take away its power. You have to do the opposite of fighting it. You have to make peace with it. You have to own it and embrace it.

Notice what happens to the yellow balloons if you stop fighting them and let them be there. They disappear. The same thing happens when you make peace with worthless. It loses power and disappears.

Now to say that you really are worthless could never be the truth. As we'll soon discover, worthy and worthless don't even exist in reality. They only exist as thoughts, but as thoughts, worthy and worthless are alive and well.

In fact, in the realm of thoughts, every judgment exists. In other words, you are everything. You are worthy and worthless, smart and stupid, brave and cowardly, lovable and unlovable, good enough and not good enough.

One moment you will feel one way and in the next moment you will feel another way.

If there is any aspect of you that you are not at peace with, the avoidance of this aspect will run your life.

To the extent that you own every aspect of yourself – the good, the bad and the ugly – you become whole and complete. Nothing can hurt you and nothing can threaten you.

In the realm of thoughts, worthless is an aspect of you. It's also part of being human. You can't get rid of it, but you can make peace with it and be *so what?* about it. The moment this happens, worthless loses its power.

You can see how this works by looking at aspects of you that you are already at peace with.

Most people are at peace with the aspect of themselves called coward. If you are one of these people, someone could call you a coward and it wouldn't bother you. You may not like it, but it wouldn't be a threat.

You would be able to say, "Yes, that's part of me. So what?" The incident would be over quickly and soon forgotten.

By being at peace with the aspect of you called coward, this area of your life works effortlessly.

You would see life clearly, and you could make

your decisions based on what works. Coward would still be an aspect of you but it would be irrelevant, and you would rarely notice it.

This is what happens when you become *so what?* about a particular aspect. It loses power.

If you were fighting the aspect of you called coward, the story would be very different. Coward would have all sorts of power.

Any circumstance that implied that you were a coward would be perceived as a threat. Automatically, you would fight and resist. You would have to prove it wasn't true.

To prove you are not a coward, you would frequently put yourself in dangerous situations. Coward would constantly be in your face, and this area of your life would be a disaster zone.

The more you run from coward, or any other aspect of yourself, the more you are guaranteed to create a life of fear, upset and suffering.

To be effective in life, you need to do the opposite of fighting these aspects. You need to embrace them. Find what they are and make peace with them.

You want to get to the place where you can say, "Yes, this is an aspect of me. So what?" You want to be able to say this and mean it.

Unfortunately, you can't just jump to *so what?* You must first go through the eye of the needle. You have to face the dragon and see that you really are this way.

The more you discover that this is, in fact, an aspect of you, the harder it is to deny it. When you can't deny it, you can't fight it. When you can't fight it, there is nothing to hold it in place. The hurt then disappears.

As you face the dragon, you automatically move to the place of *so what?* You move to *so what?* because this is the truth.

Worthless may be an aspect of you, but so is worthy. You are both worthy and worthless. They are both aspects of being human. One moment you feel one way, and in the next moment you feel the other way.

What does worthless have to do with tomorrow? Absolutely nothing. You can still have love, and you can still have your dreams come true.

The aspects that you have been resisting have never caused you any suffering. The suffering has been caused by all the things you have done to avoid feeling this way. The suffering has been caused by your fighting and resisting.

These aspects have never caused you any trouble because they don't exist. They are just thoughts. But the fighting and resisting of these aspects is very real. It's this fighting and resisting that makes life difficult.

To heal the hurt and to create a life that works, you have to remove the fighting and resisting. To do this, you have to face the dragon and see that, like it or not, worthless is an aspect of you.

This may sound like a scary thing to do, but once you see the illusion of judgment, you discover that the dragon isn't real. It only exists in your mind.

The process of healing the hurt then becomes relatively easy.

Action To Take

1. Find the aspects of you that you have been resisting. Notice that no matter what you do, these aspects keep showing up in your life. Notice that they are part of you whether you like it or not.

2. Notice how much you have been fighting these aspects. Notice that the more you fight them, the bigger they get, and the more they show up in your life.

3. Notice that these aspects have never caused you any trouble. It's all the things that you have done to avoid feeling them that have caused your suffering. It's the fighting, resisting, hanging on, withdrawing and denying that have sabotaged your life.

4. What would happen to the aspects of you that you have been resisting if you could honestly say, "Yes, these are aspects of me. So what?" Notice that they would lose their power.

Chapter 7

JUDGMENT IS AN ILLUSION

Certain aspects are threatening because we think they are real. We have been taught that there really is a thing called worthy and that there really is a thing called worthless.

We have also been taught that you need to be the thing called worthy and that you can never be the thing called worthless. You need to be a success. You can never be a failure. You need to be smart. You can never be stupid. The list goes on and on.

This is what we have been taught, and this is what we believe, but it's not the truth. These aspects don't even exist in reality. They are just illusions.

Can you go to the store and buy a package of *worthy* or *good enough*? Of course not.

JUDGMENT IS AN ILLUSION

No judgment is real.

You can search the whole world over for a *worthy* or a *good enough*, but you will never find one. If you found one, what color would it be? How much would it weigh? How big would it be?

You can't answer these questions because these aspects don't exist as things. They can only exist as thoughts, opinions and points of view.

The same is true for all judgments. Not good enough, not worth loving, failure and inadequate are only opinions.

Look at the chair you are sitting on. Is it good enough?

One person would say, "Yes, of course, the chair works fine." Another person would have a very different opinion about the same chair. "No, it's not good enough. It's the wrong size, the wrong color and the wrong style. I don't want it."

Two people have very different opinions about the same chair. One person says that the chair is good enough. Another person says it's not good enough.

What's the truth about the chair? Is it good enough or not?

The truth is neither. The chair is just the chair. Any judgment you have about the chair is just your opinion. It's something you add to the truth.

You may say that the chair is good enough, but where is the *good enough* located? Is it located in you as an opinion, or is it located in the chair? Obviously, the judgment is located in you.

Judgment can only exist in the eye of the beholder.

You can judge the chair as being one way or the other, but your judgment will never be more than a point of view. It may be a valid point of view, depending on your perspective, but it will never be the truth.

Is the chair strong or is it weak? It's neither. It's just the chair. However, if you compare it to a locomotive, the chair would be considered weak. If you compare it to a feather, the chair would be considered strong.

Are you a success or are you a failure? If you

compare yourself to a homeless person you could judge yourself as being an incredible success. If you compare yourself to a financial tycoon, you could judge yourself as being a failure.

To say that your nature is one way or another could never be the truth. You are just you. But depending on who you are comparing yourself to, your judgment could be a valid point of view.

If you had the Hope diamond, which is worth millions of dollars, and put it beside a glass of water, which would be more valuable?

If you were dying of thirst in the desert, you would certainly consider the water to be more valuable. This would be a very valid point of view. But if you were given plenty of water and placed in a jewelry store, your point of view would quickly change.

No matter what point of view you have about something, someone else will have a very different point of view about the same thing. Your point of view is just another way of looking at something. It is never the truth.

Take a moment and look at some of your judgments about people and life. Notice that with each judgment, someone else could have a very different opinion about the same thing.

Work with this concept until you can see that no judgment is ever the truth of the universe. See if you can find a judgment that is the truth. If you are honest, you won't be able to. Judgments are never more than opinions.

Notice that it would be physically impossible for you, or anyone else, to be worthless or not good enough. You could judge yourself as being this way, but never, under any circumstances, could you actually be this way.

Now look at the other side of the coin. Notice that it would also be physically impossible for you, or anyone else, to be worthy or good enough.

Worthy and worthless, good enough and not good enough, success and failure are all just judgments. They are never the truth.

Judgment can only exist in a package of opposites.

Judgment cannot exist as a thing. It can only

JUDGMENT IS AN ILLUSION

exist as a thought, and in the realm of thoughts, there is a very particular way in which judgment must show up. Judgment must show up in a package of opposites.

A good way to see this is to imagine a ladder leaning against your house. If you have *up* the ladder, you must also have *down* the ladder. Up and down must come together in the same package.

You can never have *up* without having *down*. Up can only exist if you have down to compare it to. If there is no down, there can be no up.

Up and down are two sides of the same coin. You either have both sides of the coin or no coin at all.

Never will you have only one side of the coin. Up without down cannot exist.

The same is true for all judgment. Worthy cannot exist unless you have worthless to compare it to. Success cannot exist without failure. Lovable cannot exist without unlovable.

Judgment seems real.

Do you remember the little girl who was yelled at by her mother? The moment the little girl bought the notion that she was stupid, she created the concept of smart.

Instantly, both stupid and smart became very real things to the little girl. They are not real things; they are only opinions. But to the girl, they are as real as the chair you're sitting on.

She will then go through life judging herself and others in terms of this mental concept. "This person is smart. That person is stupid. I'm smart. I'm stupid."

She will never notice that she is judging. She will think that she is observing the truth of the universe, but she's not. She is just judging.

One moment she will judge herself as being smart. In the next moment something will happen and she will judge herself as being stupid.

Neither side of the coin exists in reality, but both sides are very real in the realm of thoughts and feelings.

JUDGMENT IS AN ILLUSION

We create both sides of the coin. We then spend the rest of our lives trying to get from one side to the other, but no matter what we do, it will never be enough.

You may feel worthy for a while, but worthless will soon return. As long as you resist any aspect of yourself, that aspect will keep showing up in your life.

Action To Take

1. Notice that no matter where you look, you will never find a *worthy* or a *good enough*. These are judgments that can only exist as opinions and points of view.

2. See if you can find a judgment that is the truth of the universe. Notice that you can't. No matter what point of view you have about something, someone else will view the same thing in a very different way.

3. Notice that it would be physically impossible for you or anyone on the planet to be either worthy or worthless. These are just points of view. Work with this concept until it becomes very clear that no judgment is ever the truth. This is very important.

4. Judgment can only exist as a mental concept consisting of opposite points of view. Notice that worthy and worthless are two sides of the same coin. Notice that you can never have one side of the coin without also having the other.

Chapter 8

TWO SIDES OF THE COIN

A few years ago I worked with a man who was running from failure. In his drive to be a success, there was a point where he purchased a million-dollar home. He was so proud of himself because now he was finally a great success.

Then one Sunday afternoon, he went for a drive and discovered that his house was the smallest house in the entire neighborhood. Instantly, he was devastated. Once again, he was a worthless failure.

What happened? Did he change from one moment to the next? No. Nothing changed except his point of view. He just went from one side of the coin to the other.

One moment he viewed himself as a great success. In the next moment he viewed himself as a worthless failure.

Find a time in your life when you had a similar experience. Notice how fast it took for you to go from one side of the coin to the other. Notice how real both sides of the coin are to you.

Success and failure are only points of view, but to the man with the million-dollar house, they are much more. To him, success and failure are both very real.

Each side of the coin is total.

When the man felt like a success, he was a total success, and when he felt like a failure, he was a total failure. This is the nature of each side of the coin. Each side is total.

When you feel worthless, not good enough or whatever your issue is, the feeling is total. When you feel the opposite, that feeling is total as well. Never can you feel partly one way and partly the other. You are either on one side of the coin or the other.

It's like looking through sunglasses. Everything you see takes on the color of the lens that you look through. When you look at your life from the side of the coin called worthy, everything you see takes on the color of worthy.

When you felt your hurt as a child, you didn't feel partially worthless or not good enough. You felt totally, permanently and hopelessly that way. This is the nature of hurt.

You are also totally, permanently and hopelessly the opposite. You are both sides of the coin, and each side of the coin is total.

It's no big deal.

You are totally worthy and you are totally worthless. You are both at the same time. One moment you will feel one way, and in the next moment you will feel the other way.

Both sides of the coin are present and there is nothing you can do about it. It's also no big deal. It's just part of being human. You are both. So what? What does it have to do with tomorrow? Nothing.

Remember, the aspects that you have been resisting have never caused you any suffering. All the suffering has been caused by the things you have done to avoid feeling this way.

It's the fighting, resisting, hanging on, withdrawing and denying that has gotten you in trouble. If you could take away the fighting and resisting, your life would be great.

Here is the problem.

You are both sides of the coin. Unfortunately, we live in a world that teaches us that this is impossible.

You can't have two sides of the coin. You can only have one. And, you had better have the side considered positive. You can never have the side considered negative.

You must be worthy. You can never be worthless. You must be a success. You can never be a failure. The list goes on and on.

We've been taught that we should never have any of the aspects that we consider negative, but we do. We have all of them. They are just part of being human. It's the belief that they shouldn't be there that causes our suffering.

TWO SIDES OF THE COIN

Any time we see one of these aspects, which will be often, we will feel threatened. "No! No! I can't be worthless. Worthless is a horrible way to be. I might as well die if this is true."

We then fight these aspects like our life depends on it. We fight the aspects, and we fight all the suppressed hurt that comes with them.

We also fight any circumstance that forces us to face this hurt from the past. Instantly, we become full of fear and upset. We get tunnel vision and act in a way that can only create more suffering.

It's the fighting and resisting of these aspects that gives them all their power.

To heal this hurt and to set yourself free, you have to do the opposite of fighting them. You have to own and embrace them.

Action To Take

1. Notice that the aspects you have been resisting don't exist in reality, but they do exist in your reality. Notice how real they are to you. Notice that in one moment you feel one way, and in the next moment you feel another way.

2. Notice how fast you can go from one side of the coin to the other. Notice that whichever side of the coin you are on, the feeling is total.

3. The aspects that you have been resisting are just part of being human. You are both worthy and worthless. It's no big deal. It's the fighting and resisting that causes your suffering, not the aspects. Look in your life and see how true this is.

4. Notice how much you believe that certain aspects shouldn't be there. Notice how much you avoid feeling this hurt. Notice how much you have sabotaged your life trying to get from one side of the coin to the other.

Chapter 9

CREATE A NEW FREEDOM

Most of my life was spent running from failure. This was an aspect of myself that I did not want to face. I would do anything to avoid feeling this hurt.

In my drive to become a success, I would overspend and take unreasonable financial risks. I created a life of fear and upset. I lost my ability to see clearly, and I acted in a way that produced more and more failure.

Finally, I failed so big, I was forced to face this aspect of myself. I lost everything. I lost my investments, my office and even my home. Failure was in my face like never before.

As I looked over my life, I couldn't help but see what a failure I was. The evidence was overwhelming.

HAVE YOU SUFFERED ENOUGH?

I was forced to let in what I had feared the most. I didn't like what I saw, but I could no longer avoid it or deny it. Success was also an aspect of me, but at the time, all I could see was failure.

As I let in this aspect of myself, and as I allowed myself to feel the hurt of being this way, something very special happened. My fear of failure disappeared.

Once I saw, deep in my soul, what a failure I was, I could no longer run from it. It's like running from your shadow. You can't. When I could no longer run from it, there was nothing to give it power.

It's like the yellow balloons. The moment you stop fighting them and let them be there, they disappear. Once I stopped fighting failure, it disappeared.

I was sad for a while, but soon my whole outlook changed. The fear and upset that ran my life was no longer there. I no longer had to be a success. I could just be me. This was an incredible relief.

I hadn't been able to be me since I was four years old. I thought that in order to be okay, I had to be a success. I never dreamed that this was just some-

CREATE A NEW FREEDOM

thing I had made up. I never dreamed that it was okay to just be me.

This new freedom produced a very subtle, yet profound change in the way I lived my life. Instead of running from failure, I was able to put my focus on discovering what works in life.

Up to this point, I couldn't see what worked. In fact, what worked was irrelevant. "Don't bother me with what works. I'm not interested. Tell me how to avoid failure. I'm interested in that."

By running from failure, I lost my effectiveness. I sabotaged my dreams, and I created more failure.

Once I made peace with this aspect of myself, there was nothing to fear. Both success and failure had lost their power.

With the tunnel vision gone, I could then put my focus on creating a simple life that works. I stopped overspending, and I got out of debt.

I continued to go for my dreams, but I did so in a way that was effective. As time went on, my dreams began to come true. Now I have a life that I could never have imagined.

My life turned around the day I made peace with failure.

The same thing can happen for you. You can be free of the hurt that sabotages your life.

Fortunately, you don't have to do it the hard way. You can walk through the healing process using this book.

The first step in setting yourself free is to identify your hurt. Find the aspects of yourself that you've been fighting and resisting. What are the words of n*ot okay* that hurt the most? We will work with this more later.

The second step is to make peace with these aspects. Instead of fighting and resisting them, own and embrace them. Get to a place where you can say, "Yes, I am this way. So what?"

To get to the place of *so what?* you must first go through the eye of the needle. In other words, you have to face the dragon. You have to look deep in your soul and see how truly worthless you are. You then automatically move to the place of *so what?*

You move to *so what?* because this is the truth.

You are both worthy and worthless. So what? The aspects of you that you have been resisting are just part of being human. They don't mean a thing.

Once you face the dragon, you discover that this is an illusion that only exists in your mind. You then experience a great freedom. "What a relief. I'm a failure. How wonderful. Now I don't have to be a success any more. I can just be me."

This is the point where life starts working.

Getting to this point becomes much easier once you know how to release your suppressed hurt.

Action To Take

1. Notice what your life would be like if the aspects you have been resisting lost their power. What if you never had to be a certain way? How would it change your life? Would you like to have this freedom and peace?

2. Are you willing to face the dragon? Are you willing to release your suppressed hurt? Are you willing to own and embrace these aspects of yourself? Take a moment and see if you are willing.

3. Create within yourself the desire and the determination to face the dragon and to get to the other side of your hurt.

Chapter 10

RELEASE YOUR SUPPRESSED HURT

On the surface, we fight and resist certain circumstances, but at a deeper level, we are avoiding something inside of ourselves. We don't want to feel all the suppressed hurt that our circumstances reactivate.

It's the automatic avoidance of this hurt that gets us into trouble. If you were free of this hurt, there would be nothing to fear and nothing to avoid. You would see life clearly, and you would be very effective.

Notice how different your life would be if all your suppressed hurt were gone.

Fortunately, the process of releasing this suppressed emotion is relatively simple.

Look at little children. Little children are masters at healing hurt. When a child feels hurt, the child cries. Then, after the child finishes crying, the hurt is all gone.

Little children are able to release their hurt because they do something that we don't notice. They are totally willing to feel their emotions.

The key word here is *willing*. Little children feel their hurt willingly. When you feel your hurt willingly, you allow the hurt to run its course. It then loses power and disappears.

To see this in your life, find a time when you were hurt and you allowed yourself to cry. Then, after you cried your last tear, you felt a wonderful freedom. This will be a time when you felt your hurt willingly.

This is also the natural process for healing hurt. We are created with the ability to release all our negative emotions. All we have to do is feel them willingly, like a child.

Unfortunately, we relate to hurt in a way that makes this almost impossible.

Instead of allowing ourselves to feel our emotion, we have been taught to fight it. "Big boys and girls

RELEASE YOUR SUPPRESSED HURT

don't cry. If you want to cry, I'll give you something to cry about."

By fighting our hurt, we stop the natural healing process. Instead of letting the hurt run its course and disappear, we fight it and keep it inside. Instead of releasing the hurt, we suppress it and give it more power.

The irony is that no matter what you do to avoid your hurt, you can't get away from it. You will continue to feel it whether you are willing to or not.

This is the nature of hurt. When you're hurt, you're hurt. You don't have a choice whether you are going to feel it. You will. Your only choice is this: Are you going to feel your hurt willingly, like a child, or are you going to fight it and keep it inside?

Now, you may feel like you have been willing to feel your hurt, but have you been willing to feel the hurt of being totally worthless, not good enough or whatever your core issue is? You probably haven't. If you were, you would have healed your hurt years ago.

The hurt of feeling worthless is a hurt that we fight with all of our might. We fight this hurt because, subconsciously, it's a serious threat to our survival.

"I can't be worthless. Worthless is a horrible way to be. If I'm worthless, I might as well just die."

We will do almost anything to avoid feeling this hurt, but no matter what we do, it keeps coming back; and the more we fight it, the more we are forced to experience it in our lives.

This may sound like bad news, but it's not. It's good news. The hurt keeps showing up in your life so that it can be experienced like a child and then be released.

The human body is constantly trying to purge itself of impurities. If you get a splinter in your finger and can't find it, the splinter will eventually work its way to the surface so that it can be removed.

The same thing happens with suppressed hurt. Every time you get upset or have a wave of hurt, your suppressed hurt has been brought to the surface so that it can purge itself.

But instead of feeling the emotion like a child and letting it go, we fight it. We push it back inside so we don't have to feel it.

Suppressing hurt is like pushing the splinter back

RELEASE YOUR SUPPRESSED HURT

inside so we don't have to look at it. Pushing back your hurt only creates more pain.

If you want to be free inside and have your life be as great as it can be, stop suppressing your hurt. Release it.

Use every upset and every wave of hurt as an opportunity for more healing. Instead of fighting the hurt, allow yourself to feel it willingly, like a child. Cry if you can. Let it come and let it go.

Crying is the most powerful way to release emotion. Develop your ability to cry.

Sometimes you may feel the hurt, but there aren't any tears. When this happens, fake the tears. This primes the pump and allows the tears to become real.

If the tears don't become real, that's okay. Faking the tears and actively creating the emotion is still sufficient to release it.

The key to releasing your hurt is to get into it with all your might. Feel it with gusto. Actively create it. Exaggerate it. Make it bigger than it really is. Feel it deliberately and intentionally.

Reach inside and pull it out. Feel the hurt because you want to, rather than because you are forced to.

Keep telling yourself, "It's okay to feel the hurt. It's okay." Let the hurt come and let it go. Cry as hard as you can.

Cry the hurt of your circumstances, and cry the hurt of being worthless or whatever your issue is.

While you are crying the hurt of your issue, look for the words that hurt the most. Look for your hurt. Dive in to it and feel it with all of your might.

By actively and deliberately feeling your hurt, you are doing the opposite of fighting it. You are feeling it willingly. This allows the hurt to come and go quickly.

Use every opportunity you can to find and release more hurt.

You may feel that there is so much hurt, that if you were to allow yourself to feel it all, the hurt would overpower you and you would never recover. This may be your fear, but it's not the truth.

RELEASE YOUR SUPPRESSED HURT

Hurt is just a feeling. There is nothing about hurt that can harm you.

It is only when you fight the hurt that you experience it as pain. When you allow yourself to feel it willingly like a child, the same hurt is experienced as healing.

So let the hurt come and let it go. You may cry lots of tears, but once the hurt is released, you will experience a new freedom in life.

Do everything you can to release your suppressed hurt.

Action To Take

1. Be willing to feel your hurt and the feelings of being *not okay*. Keep telling yourself, "It's okay to feel the hurt. It's okay." Let it come and let it go.

2. Notice that you don't have a choice about whether you are going to feel your hurt. You will. Your only choice is to feel it willingly, and let it go like a child, or fight it and keep it inside.

3. When you feel your hurt, cry as hard as you can. Exaggerate it. Get into it with all your might. This is the opposite of fighting it. By actively creating your hurt, you allow it to come and go quickly.

4. Cry the hurt of your circumstances and cry the hurt of feeling worthless, not good enough or whatever your issue is. Do everything you can to release your suppressed hurt.

5. Notice the freedom and inner peace that you experience after you release your hurt. Notice how painful it is when you fight it.

Chapter 11

START THE HEALING PROCESS

Now it's time to start the healing process. You have a unique opportunity to be free of the hurt that has been sabotaging your life. You can have a freedom and a peace of mind that you haven't experienced in years.

The process for healing your hurt and setting yourself free is relatively easy, but it takes some diligence. You can read through the next few chapters and understand how the process works, but this won't be enough to change your life.

To change your life, you need more than understanding. You need to experience the healing deep inside. To accomplish this, put yourself in the hurt and walk through the steps on an emotional level, rather than an intellectual level.

Let's start the process by looking at the nature of your hurt. As a little child, you couldn't help but buy the notion that you were worthless, not good enough or some other form of *not okay*.

You also decided that you were totally, permanently and hopelessly this way. Every bit of your soul was this way. This is the degree of hurt that needs to be healed.

To heal this hurt and to have it lose its power, you have to do the opposite of fighting it. You have to face it, let it in, and own it. Here are the steps:

1. Find the specific hurt that runs your life.

2. Feel the hurt of being this way.

3. Look at your life and find the evidence to prove that you are this way.

4. Keep in mind that being this way is also *so what*?

To the extent that you own any aspect of yourself, it becomes irrelevant and ceases to run your life.

START THE HEALING PROCESS

Find the specific hurt that runs your life.

The first step in the healing process is to find what the hurt is. Look for the words of *not okay* that hurt the most. The more painful the words, the closer you are to your hurt.

What are the aspects of you that you are avoiding? Are you avoiding the hurt of feeling worthless, not good enough, not worth loving or failure? Keep looking for the words that most accurately describe your hurt.

You will have lots of issues, but there is usually one main core issue that runs your life. This is the hurt that you want to look for.

Once you discover the aspects of you that you have been resisting, you won't like it. Just the thought of being this way will be enough to send cold chills up and down your spine. You may even want to deny it. "I know I'm not worthless. I'm definitely not a failure."

If there are any words that you are denying, look there first. You have probably found your core issue. You wouldn't be defensive unless you felt there was something to be defensive about.

Keep looking for the word or words that hurt the most. We'll look at this more in the next chapter.

Feel the hurt of being this way.

This is one of the most important steps in the healing process. Feeling your hurt is the key to healing it.

Your hurt has power only because you fight it. When you stop fighting your hurt and allow yourself to feel it willingly like a child, the hurt runs its course and disappears.

Look for your hurt. Be willing to feel it. Let it come and let it go. Keep telling yourself, "It's okay. It's okay." Feel the hurt of being worthless, not good enough, not worth loving or whatever your issue is.

Cry your hurt as hard as you can. Reach in and pull it out. Get into the emotion of it. Feel it fully. Exaggerate it.

The more you face your hurt and feel it willingly, like a child, the more you are able to release it.

Keep in mind, hurt is just a feeling. It can't hurt you.

Look at your life and find the evidence to prove that you are this way.

There is a wonderful freedom that takes place once you discover that the aspects you have been resisting are just part of being human. You gain this freedom by making peace with these aspects.

The best way to do this is to look at your life and see all the evidence to prove that you are this way. You don't have to like it. You just have to tell the truth. This is an aspect of you. The more you discover that this is true, the more impossible it is to fight it.

Now this is not something that we want to do. We do not want to look at this aspect of ourselves. But if you want to heal your hurt, this is what you have to do.

To find the evidence, put yourself in the hurt of feeling worthless or whatever your issue is. This is important because if you look at your life intellectually, you may not see any evidence. If you put yourself in the hurt, you will see the evidence everywhere.

So put yourself in the hurt and look at your life. Look at all your upsets. Each upset will be more proof that you really are this way. Keep looking for more and more evidence to prove that this is true. Keep looking until you can clearly see your worthlessness.

While you are looking, notice if you keep jumping to the side of the coin that you consider positive. If you are, this will be a subconscious attempt to avoid your hurt.

The positive side is also an aspect of you, but that side of the coin isn't causing you any trouble. To heal your hurt, keep your focus on the side of the coin that you have been avoiding.

Keep in mind that being this way is also so what?

As you let in the fact that you are this way, you soon discover that being this way is quite irrelevant. You are also the opposite. You are also an incredibly wonderful human being.

Both sides of the coin are aspects of you. So what? What does this have to do with tomorrow? Absolutely nothing. So give yourself a break and allow yourself to be human. Notice how freeing this is.

Action To Take

1. Make sure you take the time to walk through the healing process on an emotional level rather than on an intellectual level. A mere understanding of how the process works won't change your life.

2. Create within yourself the commitment and the determination to do whatever it takes to discover and heal the hurt that runs your life. Walk through the healing process like your life depends on it. It does.

3. Look for the aspects of you that you have been avoiding and let in the hurt of being this way. Notice that these really are aspects of you. Allow yourself to feel the hurt and keep moving toward *so what?*

4. Remember, the aspects that you have been resisting are not the only aspects of you. They are only a few of millions. They just happen to be big ones because your resistance has magnified them out of proportion. You are also an incredibly wonderful human being.

Chapter 12

Find Your Hurt

The first step in the healing process is to discover, as specifically as possible, what your core issue is. What are the aspects of you that you have been avoiding and resisting?

Use the sections in this chapter to discover what those aspects are. Each section will look at a different area of your life. To determine how much power a particular aspect has over you, notice how you would feel if you really were this way?

The more you resist the thought of being a particular way, the closer you are to your hurt. Keep looking for the word or words that hurt the most. Be as specific as possible.

As much as you can, put yourself in the hurt. This is the best to find what the specific hurt is.

FIND YOUR HURT

To more accurately describe your hurt, you may want to use a combination of words. You may want to use combinations like these: worthless failure, hopelessly unlovable, stupid loser, or weak, whiny wimp.

While you are looking for your hurt, make sure you forward the healing process. Let in the hurt of being this way and look over your life to see all the evidence that proves that you are this way.

Keep in mind that being this way is also *so what?*

Now it's time to find the words that most accurately describe your hurt.

A list of common core issues

Look over the following list of common core issues and make a list of the words that hurt the most. If possible, have someone read them to you. Hearing an issue is much more reactivating than reading one.

Listen to each word as though it accurately describes who you are.

HAVE YOU SUFFERED ENOUGH?

How would you feel if you really were:

unlovable	can't cut it
undesirable	don't have what it takes
not worth loving	incompetent
worthless	screwed up
not worth respecting	something is wrong
have no value	with you
have deficit value	can't do anything right
no good	stupid
not good enough	unstable
not good enough	defective
to be loved	not acceptable
don't measure up	weak
inadequate	helpless
inferior	clingy
insufficient	needy
less than	a wimp
useless	a coward
a nothing	irresponsible
insignificant	unreliable
unimportant	lazy
don't count	self-centered
don't matter	inconsiderate
a throwaway	selfish
a nobody	dishonest
a loser	bad
a failure	wrong

FIND YOUR HURT

evil
repulsive
heartless
horrible person

ugly
fat
a slut
just like your parents

What are your upsets?

Make a list of every major hurt and upset that you have had during your life. Be as specific as you can. What happened? You don't need a detailed explanation. Just write down enough to remind you of the incident.

See if you can come up with at least twelve times when you have been hurt or upset. The longer your list, the easier it will be to find and heal your hurt.

After you complete your list, look for the hurt that is under each upset.

For each incident, go to the moment the incident began and find the specific circumstance that you were upset about. What happened?

Then put yourself in the hurt of the incident and ask yourself the question, "What does that circumstance say about me?"

If someone left you, this could say that you are unlovable or not worth loving. If you got fired from your job, this could say that you are not good enough or a failure. Find the words that hurt the most.

As you work with your list of upsets, you will discover that the same aspects keep showing up. Make a note of these aspects and keep looking for words that are even more painful.

Once you think you have found your hurt, ask yourself, "If I really am this way, what would that say about me?" Use this question to see if there is a hurt that is even deeper than the one you have found.

How is your relationship with your parents?

If you have had a difficult relationship with one or both of your parents, this is probably where your hurt began.

Go back in time and allow yourself to feel the hurt that you experienced as a child. What did your parents imply about you in their actions and in their words? Did they say that you were worthless or not good enough?

How would you feel if everything your parents said or implied about you were the truth? You really are this way. How would you feel, if it were true, that you are so worthless and not good enough that you deserved everything they did to you?

If this is a painful thought, or if you say that this isn't true, you have probably found the core issue that runs your life. Find the words that most accurately describe this hurt and keep looking.

What do you resist in your parents?

How would you feel if you were exactly like your parents? For most people, this would be a very uncomfortable thought. Notice if this is uncomfortable for you.

If you resist certain aspects of your parents, you will resist these aspects wherever they show up. You will resist them in other people, and you will resist them in yourself.

What are the aspects of your parents that you resist? List every one of them. Each one will be an aspect of you that you are resisting.

You may not do the same things that your parents do, but this doesn't mean that the aspects aren't in you. Notice how much you strive to be the opposite. You wouldn't try to be the opposite unless you were trying to get away from something.

Let in the hurt of being this way and look in your life to see all the evidence to prove that this is, indeed, an aspect of you.

Once you see that you are just like your parents, your resistance toward them gets replaced with love and compassion.

What are your fears?

Fears are very similar to upsets. The main difference is that in a fear, you are avoiding a future event. In an upset, you are avoiding a past or present event. Both fear and upsets are created by the avoidance of some hurt.

If you have a fear of losing someone, it looks like you are avoiding the loss of the person. But in reality, you are avoiding all the hurt that would be reactivated if the person was missing from your life.

In other words, we don't really avoid circumstances. We avoid the hurt that the circumstances reactivate.

Another way to find your hurt is to make a list of your fears and look for what you are really avoiding. What would you have to experience if your fears came true? What would those circumstances say about you?

Has rejection, abandonment or failure been an issue for you?

Would an incredibly wonderful person be rejected or abandoned? No way. Not according to the hurt.

So what kind of person would this happen to? What would it say about you if you were rejected or abandoned? For most people, this would say that you are unlovable or not worth loving.

Notice how painful this would be if it were true.

Now look and see if you also have an issue with failure. Not worth loving and failure usually come together. This is because they are both elements of worthless.

Failure is being worthless in the area of producing results. Not worth loving is being worthless in the area of relationships.

Would it be painful if you really were worthless and had no value? This is the core issue that most people run from. See if this is more painful than not worth loving or failure. Go with the words that hurt the most.

What are you driven toward?

We are never driven toward something. We are always driven from something. We are driven to escape the aspects of ourselves that we consider to be horrible and to become the aspects that we think we should be.

If you are driven to be a success, you are running from failure. If you have to be accepted, you

==FIND YOUR HURT==

==are running from some form of being not acceptable. If you have to be right, you are running from being wrong and, more accurately, being stupid.==

By discovering what you are driven toward, you can find what you are driven from. So take a moment and find what you are driven toward. What do you need for your happiness?

Then look for the opposite. What hurt would you have to experience if you could never have what you are driven toward? What would those circumstances say about you?

What are you denying?

In the realm of thinking, every judgment exists. You are worthy and worthless; smart and stupid; good and bad. You are everything.

If there is any aspect that you deny having, this will be an aspect of you that you are resisting. You wouldn't deny it unless you thought it was a horrible way to be.

To get past the denial, notice all the hurt that you would have to feel if you really were this way.

It's the subconscious avoidance of this hurt that brings the denial.

Allow yourself to feel this hurt. Then look for evidence to prove that this really is an aspect of you.

What is your core issue?

Now go back and review the list of common core issues. See if any new words stand out. Then review the entire chapter and select the word or words that most accurately describe your hurt.

You may have several aspects that are particularly painful. For example, you may have the hurt of worthless and also the hurt of inadequate. Select the words that hurt the most.

You can work with all the aspects later, but for now, find the hurt that is the most painful. Once you find the words that describe this hurt, you are ready for the next step.

Action To Take

1. Use this chapter to find the hurt that runs your life. Keep looking for the words that most accurately describe your hurt. Be as specific as possible. The more painful the words, the more they run your life.

2. While you are looking, let in the hurt of being this way. Allow yourself to feel the hurt willingly, like a child. Cry as much as you can. This is the most powerful way to release your suppressed hurt.

3. Put yourself in the hurt of feeling this way and look over your life. Find all the evidence to prove that you are this way. Get to the place where you see the evidence everywhere. This is an aspect of you. The more you let this in, the more impossible it is to run from it.

4. Pay special attention to any aspect that you deny having. You wouldn't need to deny it unless you were fighting it. Keep in mind that being this way is also, *so what*?

Chapter 13

FACE THE DRAGON

The next step in the healing process is to make peace with the aspects of you that you've been resisting. As you do this, the aspects lose their power and your hurt disappears.

The following questions will walk you through a process that can make this happen. To be most effective, get in touch with your hurt before you start the exercise.

Recall the specific aspect that you are going to work with. Then notice the hurt associated with being this way. Get in touch with this hurt. Then start answering the questions.

Work with each question until you can say "yes" and mean it. Take your time and allow yourself to experience the truth of each answer.

While you are walking through the exercise, continue to let in the hurt of being this way, and look for evidence to prove that you are this way.

- Notice the years and years of hurt associated with being this way. Is this a hurt that you have not wanted to experience?

- Is this a hurt that you would do almost anything to avoid feeling?

- Do you see the enormous amount of energy and effort that you have spent trying to avoid feeling this hurt?

- No matter what you have done to avoid it, doesn't this hurt keep showing up in your life, over and over again?

- Notice that the more you have avoided this hurt, the more you have had to experience it. Do you see that this is true?

- Would you like to heal this hurt?

- Are you willing to stop fighting it?

- Are you willing to feel all the hurt of being this way?

- Are you willing to feel this hurt, like a child, and let it come and let it go?

Notice that you don't have a choice about whether you are going to feel this hurt. You will. Your only choice is this: Are you going to feel it willingly, like a child, and let it go, or are you going to fight it and keep it inside?

Allow yourself to experience all the hurt of being this way. Cry if you can. Crying is the most powerful way to release your hurt. Do this now if you can.

Create within yourself a desire to look for more of this hurt so that you can find and heal more of it. The more you look for your hurt, the more it disappears. This is the opposite of running from it.

- Can you see a lifetime of incidents where you have felt this hurt?

- Hasn't every incident been more proof that, down deep, you really are this way?

- Are you willing to discover that this is the truth? You really are this way.

- Can you look in your life and see a lifetime of evidence to prove that this is true?

This is the most important part of the healing process. To the degree that you know you are this way, you can no longer run from it. The aspect loses power and your hurt disappears.

Put yourself in the hurt of feeling this way and look at your life. Search for evidence to prove that this is truly an aspect of you.

Look at all the times when you felt the hurt of being this way. Each time will be more proof. Let in the fact that you are this way, and allow yourself to feel your hurt.

Get to the place where you can see the evidence everywhere you look.

If you are fighting the notion that you are this way, notice that your resistance doesn't make the aspect go away. Notice that this aspect is still there and that your resistance is totally irrelevant. This is still an aspect of you.

- Now that you look, isn't this is an aspect of you?

- Isn't this true whether you like it or not?

- Even if you hate it and deny that it exists, isn't this still an aspect of you?

- Would it be accurate to say that you have spent most of your life fighting this aspect, trying to make it go away?

- Do you see how much you have suffered and sabotaged your life trying to get rid of this aspect?

- After all you have done to get rid of it, do you see that this aspect is still there?

- Do you see that by your resisting, you have only made it stronger?

- Are you now willing to stop fighting this aspect of you and make peace with it?

- Do you now give this aspect full permission to be in your life?

Notice that, once again, you don't have a choice. This aspect is going to be there whether you like it or not. You can either fight it and give it more power, or you can make peace with it and have it lose power.

- Are you willing to surrender to the truth of its existence?

- Do you now give this aspect full permission to be in your life forever, to never, ever go away?

- Do you see that much of your life has been spent running from this aspect, trying to become the opposite?

- Can you see how much you have suffered and sacrificed, trying to become the opposite? Can you see how much you have sabotaged your life trying to be a certain way?

- Notice that no matter how hard you have worked to become a certain way, you haven't gotten there yet. Do you see that you never can?

You can never have only one side of the coin. Trying to have worthy without worthless is like chasing a rainbow. You can never get there, but you can certainly create a lot of suffering in the attempt.

- Do you see the enormous pressure that you have put on yourself, having to be a certain way?

- Can you imagine the incredible freedom and relief

that you would experience if you never had to be the opposite way?

- Would you like to have this freedom?

- Are you willing to give up having to be a certain way? Are you willing to give it up forever, and just be you?

- Do you feel a difference inside? Do you experience more freedom and peace? Do you feel more able to be yourself?

Keep working with this until you get to a place where you experience a great freedom. "Oh, how wonderful. I'm worthless. What a relief. Now I don't have to prove I'm worthy any more. I can just be me."

Take the time to do this exercise with every aspect that you have been resisting.

Keep in mind that being a certain way doesn't mean a thing. "I am this way. So what? I'm also the opposite. What does this have to do with tomorrow? Absolutely nothing. I can still do what works, and I can still have a great life."

Action To Take

1. Use the questions in this chapter to make peace with the aspects of you that you've been resisting. Work with each question until you can say "yes" and mean it.

2. Do everything you can to see that you really are this way. Let in the hurt and look for all the evidence to prove that this is true. You really are this way. Let it in.

3. While you are letting in the hurt, keep moving toward *so what?* Get to the place where you experience the freedom of no longer having to be a certain way.

4. Do this exercise with all the aspects that you have been avoiding. Make peace with every one of them.

Chapter 14

STEPS FOR MORE HEALING

How does it feel now to be worthless, not good enough or whatever your core issue is? Do you feel a new freedom? Do you feel more at peace? Do you feel more able to be yourself?

To the degree that you make peace with these aspects, they literally disappear from your life, along with all the destructive behavior that they generate.

Use your upsets for more healing.

To the degree that you don't own a particular aspect or to the degree that you resist it, that aspect is guaranteed to come back. It will come back in the form of an upset.

STEPS FOR MORE HEALING

So, every time you get upset, you have an opportunity to find and heal more of the hurt that runs your life.

Take the following steps whenever you get upset:

1. Go to the moment the upset began and find the specific circumstance that you are resisting. What happened? Be as specific as possible.

2. Ask yourself, "Why can't I be at peace with what happened? What do those circumstances say about me?"

3. Find the aspects of you that you are resisting and let in the hurt of being this way. Cry as hard as you can. Actively create the hurt. Exaggerate it. Let it come and let it go.

4. Look over your life and see all the evidence to prove that you are this way. "I'm a worthless failure. I hate it, but I can't deny it. This is definitely an aspect of me." Let it in.

5. Allow yourself to feel the hurt willingly, like a child. Then gently move to *so what?* Keep in mind that you are also the other side of the coin. Allow yourself be human.

Every time you own a little more of an aspect that you have been resisting and every time you allow yourself to feel more of your suppressed hurt, you take the healing a little deeper. You gain more peace of mind and life works a little better.

Go through life continually looking for more upsets. Keep a log and write down every upset that you have. Then take each one and walk through the healing process.

Sometimes you will find the hurt quickly. Sometimes it takes longer, but keep looking. At first, you will work with the obvious issues. Then, as life goes on, you will discover new core issues and deeper levels of old ones.

As you continue to work with this, your upsets will become noticeably less frequent and far less severe. You soon reach a point where you are rarely upset.

Let go of your issue.

Do you have any resistance to letting go of your issue? Usually, there is a part of us that doesn't want to let go of the hurt. If this is true for you, you are certainly not alone.

So why would we want to hang on to something that causes so much pain and suffering? We hang on to our hurt because it's the perfect excuse.

As long as we have our issue, we don't have to be responsible for our lives. "What can you expect of me? I'm just worthless."

Notice how you have used your core issue as an excuse in life. Notice how this excuse has held you back and has kept you from going for your dreams.

Now notice the explanation and story you have surrounding your issue. This happened and that happened. Your parents caused this and your circumstances caused that.

This explanation and story about your life is also an excuse for not taking action. "I can't do great things because I have this past." Notice how this story keeps you from moving forward.

Now see if you are willing to give up both your issue and the story surrounding it. Are you willing to take full responsibility for your life?

Are you now willing to give up your explanation for why your life is the way it is? Are you now willing to let go of your issue? Are you willing to move forward in your life?

Keep working with this until you no longer need either the story or the issue.

Relive your old upsets.

Make a list of your most painful upsets. Then, for each upset, go back in time to the moment the incident began. Then relive it. Walk through the incident, moment-by-moment, step-by-step, detail-by-detail.

As you walk through the incident, allow yourself to feel all the feelings and emotions of the event. Cry the hurt of the circumstances and cry the hurt of feeling worthless or whatever your issue is. Let the hurt come, and let it go like a child.

When you finish walking through the incident, walk through it again. Keep walking through the incident, over and over, until all the suppressed hurt is gone.

Do this exercise with every incident in your past where you still have suppressed emotion. Then go through life looking for opportunities to release more hurt.

STEPS FOR MORE HEALING

Be willing for your fears to happen.

Find your biggest fears and give them permission to happen. If you are resisting the possibility of someone leaving you, imagine that person in front of you, and give the person permission to go.

"I let you go. I am willing for you to be with another person." Find the words that are the most threatening and say them aloud. Use the words to reactivate your hurt so you can release it.

Keep saying the words over and over until you can say them and mean them without any emotion. This is a powerful way to release more of your suppressed hurt.

Work with this until you are willing for anything to happen.

Tell a friend of your worthlessness.

Get with a friend and tell the person all the aspects of you that you have been resisting. Then give the person all the evidence to prove that you really are this way.

This exercise is important because if you can't talk about your issues, you can't own them. By forcing yourself to talk about them, your issues lose even more power.

While you are revealing these aspects of you, be light about it. Be playful. The more you can laugh about your issues, the more insignificant they become.

Get to the place where you are willing for anyone to know this about you. It's a wonderful freedom when you don't have to hide it anymore.

If you feel stuck or if you have difficulty finding or healing a core issue, call our office and have a telephone consulting session with me or a member of my staff.

This is a great way to get to the other side of an issue. Our phone number is (713) 520-5370.

As you make peace with yourself, you restore your ability to flow with life. Instead of resisting, you discover solutions. You become more creative and far more effective.

Making peace with yourself is the key to creating a life that works.

ACTION TO TAKE

1. Notice that the aspects of you that you have been resisting no longer have the same power. Notice that they never will. This is because you have started the process of making peace with them.

2. Every upset is an opportunity for more healing. Use your upsets to discover new aspects of you that you have been resisting, and to discover deeper levels of old ones. Use the steps in this chapter to find and heal the hurt that is under each upset.

3. Keep a log and, as you go through life, write down every upset that you have. Then take each upset and walk through the healing process. The more you work with your upsets, the more they disappear from your life.

4. Use the exercises in this chapter to take the healing even deeper. Relive your old upsets. Be willing for your fears to happen and tell a friend of your worthlessness.

Chapter 15

BE FREE OF GUILT

To make peace with yourself, you need to make peace with the aspects of you that you have been resisting. You also need to be free of guilt.

This is particularly important because guilt reinforces the feelings of being *not okay*. If you did all those horrible things, that proves you are not good enough, worthless and so on.

Guilt keeps your suppressed hurt in place and keeps you from flowing with life. You feel undeserving and hold yourself back. To have your life be as great as it can be, you need to be free of your guilt.

The key to releasing guilt is to recognize that we all go through life doing the very best we can with the extremely limited awareness that we have.

BE FREE OF GUILT

Unfortunately, what we have is seldom enough. As a result, we make mistakes. Sometimes we make big ones.

Making mistakes is part of the human process. That is how we learn. Every time you make a mistake you discover a little more about life. You then become a little wiser and more aware.

If you look, the most valuable lessons you've ever learned are those that you could only have learned the hard way.

Everyone makes mistakes. What matters is what you do with them. If you recognize that you did the very best you could with where you were at the time, you would be free inside. When you believe you should have been wiser than you were, you have guilt.

Guilt is never caused by what happened. Guilt is something that you add later with hindsight.

At the moment of your actions, you were doing exactly what you thought you should do. You were acting totally consistent with the limited awareness that you had at the time.

HAVE YOU SUFFERED ENOUGH?

We create guilt to punish ourselves. We think that if we just punish ourselves enough, this will somehow make up for what we did. We are our own judge and jury.

Maybe now you have suffered enough. Ask yourself, are you willing to be forgiven? Are you willing to be free of your guilt? Have you punished yourself enough?

If you are ready to be free of your guilt, make a list of everything you have ever done that you feel guilty about. Then use the following questions to release your guilt. Work with one guilt at a time.

- Did you do that thing for which you have guilt? Face what you did, and allow yourself to feel your hurt.

- Now go back in time to the moment you did whatever you did. At that moment, didn't you have a very particular state of mind? Didn't you see life in a very particular way?

- Didn't you act totally consistent with that state of mind and the way you saw life at that moment?

- If you knew then what you know today – if you had a different state of mind – wouldn't you have been able to interact very differently?

- You didn't know then what you know today, did you? You only knew what you knew, and that wasn't enough.

Five years from now you are going to be much wiser and more aware than you are today. But the wisdom you are going to have five years from now doesn't do you any good today. Today, you only have the wisdom that you have.

Likewise, the wisdom you have today didn't do you any good back then. Back then, you only knew what you knew. If you had today's wisdom, you could have operated very differently, but you didn't.

"But I should have known." Nonsense. How could you possibly have known more than you did? Even if you thought you knew, you didn't know enough to change your actions. You certainly didn't know the consequences like you do now.

If you look, you did the very best you could with the very limited awareness that you had. If you had a different state of mind, you would have been able to handle your situation very differently, but you didn't. You only had what you had at the time.

- Didn't you do the very best you could with the limited awareness that you had at the time?

- Are you willing to experience all the hurt from what you did?

One of the main reasons we have guilt is so we don't have to feel this hurt. Once you are willing to feel this hurt, you no longer need your guilt.

You can forgive yourself and still be sad. You can also regret what you did. You just don't have to punish yourself anymore.

- Are you willing to forgive yourself for not knowing and for not being wiser and more aware? You might as well.

- Are you willing to forgive yourself for acting consistent with your limited awareness?

BE FREE OF GUILT

- Are you willing to forgive yourself for the damage you caused as a result of your not knowing?

- Do you now totally forgive yourself for not being wiser and more aware, and for doing whatever you did? Do you now let go of all guilt for your actions, just because you say so?

Forgiveness is a choice and a declaration. "I forgive myself. I'm sad and I regret what I did, but I forgive myself. I forgive myself just because I say so."

Sometimes you can release your guilt in an instant. That's how long you took to create it. Sometimes, releasing a guilt takes longer. Sometimes you have to forgive yourself over and over, until your guilt is finally gone.

If releasing a guilt seems difficult, you are probably avoiding the hurt of a core issue. To find what that issue is, ask yourself, "If I did that horrible thing, what would that say about me?"

Find the core issue that you have been avoiding and let in the hurt of being this way. When you finish facing your hurt, see if you are willing to forgive yourself for having this aspect. If you are, walk through the questions again.

Do whatever it takes to release your guilt. Forgive yourself for everything you have ever done from the time you were born until now. Work with each item of guilt until all your guilt is gone.

As you become free of guilt, you become more at peace. You become less judgmental and more forgiving. You feel better about yourself and better about life.

ACTION TO TAKE

1. Notice how much you have suffered from your guilt. Have you been punished enough? See if you are willing to be free of all your guilt?

2. List everything you have ever done that you feel guilty about. Then use the questions in this chapter to release your guilt. Work with one incident at a time.

3. Notice that if you were wiser and more aware you would have been able to handle your situation in a very different way, but you weren't wiser and more aware. You only knew what you knew.

4. Notice that you have always done the best you could with the very limited awareness that you had at the time. Forgive yourself for not being wiser and more aware.

5. Work with this chapter until you are totally free of all guilt.

Chapter 16

LET GO OF RESENTMENT

Another way we create suffering is through resentment. When you have resentment, part of you closes down. You lose your aliveness and your peace of mind. You become bitter and less able to express your love.

You also make your life more difficult. When you resent someone, you are saying, "I strongly dislike you." This destroys the experience of love. The other person then gets upset and becomes resentful toward you.

Then you get more upset and become more critical toward the other person. Then the other person gets more resentful toward you. You soon create a cycle of conflict that produces needless upset and suffering.

LET GO OF RESENTMENT

To end the conflict and restore your peace of mind, you need to release your resentment.

Ironically, when you resent someone, you are the only one who really suffers. The other person is out enjoying life while you are stuck with your upset.

Notice the price you pay for your resentment. Notice how much freedom, aliveness and peace of mind you have lost.

Letting go of a resentment is not for the benefit of the other person. Letting go of a resentment is for you. You release your resentment so you can heal your hurt and get on with your life.

We think that resentment is caused by another person, but it's not. No one has the power to create a resentment in you. Only you can do that.

You create your own resentment. You create resentment in a subconscious attempt to avoid your hurt.

Resentment is the forceful blaming of someone else. That person is the problem, the cause, the fault. Not you. You forcefully blame the other person so you don't have to look at yourself.

If you were to look at yourself, you would have to experience all the hurt from what happened. You would have to feel the hurt of being not good enough, not worth loving, or whatever your core issue is.

It's the subconscious attempt to avoid this hurt that creates your resentment.

A good example of this took place several years ago. Karen resented Roger for leaving her. Under her anger and resentment, Karen had a deep hurt of feeling not worth loving. This was a hurt that she had spent most of her life avoiding.

When Roger left, this suppressed hurt was reactivated. His leaving proved that she wasn't worth loving. To avoid this hurt, Karen had to blame Roger for what had happened.

She couldn't dare face the possibility that Roger had left because of her. Karen was in turmoil because of her resentment and the suppressed feelings of being not worth loving.

When Karen came to see me, she faced her hurt and healed her core issue. Once this happened, she no longer needed her resentment. She forgave Roger and set herself free inside. She restored her peace of mind.

You can do the same thing. The process for releasing resentment is very simple.

The first step is to find and heal the hurt that you are avoiding. To do this, take the following action:

1. Find the specific circumstances that you are resisting. What happened?

2. Determine what those circumstances say about you? Do they say that you are worthless, not good enough or not worth loving? Find the words that hurt the most.

3. Then let in the hurt. Feel the hurt of the circumstances and the hurt of being this way. Cry as hard as you can. Let the hurt come and let it go.

4. Look in your life and see all the evidence to prove that you are this way. Keep in mind that this is also *so what*?

As you let in the hurt, the need to blame disappears and the resentment loses power.

The next step is to see that the person you resent was doing the very best he or she could with his or her extremely limited awareness. This will create some compassion for the person.

Use the following questions to let go of your resentment. Work with one resentment at a time.

- Are you willing to be free of your resentment? Have you suffered enough?

- Are you willing to feel all the hurt associated with what happened? Are you willing to feel all the hurt of being worthless, not good enough or whatever your issue is?

- Now take a good look at the person you resent. Doesn't this person have a very particular state of mind and way of seeing life?

- Doesn't this person act totally consistent with his or her limited awareness?

- If the person was wiser and more aware, wouldn't he or she be able to act in a very different way?

- Do you see that the person isn't wiser and more

aware? Do you see that this person has a very limited awareness?

- Are you willing to forgive this person for not knowing, for not being wiser and more aware?

- Isn't this person doing the very best he or she can with his or her limited view of life?

- Are you willing to forgive the person for acting consistent with his or her limited ability?

- Are you willing to forgive the person for the damage that was done as a result of this limited awareness?

- Do you now let go of all resentment for the person, just because you say so?

The moment you release your resentment, you physically feel the return of your aliveness. You restore your peace of mind, your compassion and your ability to love.

Work with this chapter until you are totally free of all resentment.

If you have trouble releasing a resentment, find the hurt that you are avoiding. What do those circumstances say about you? Then let in the hurt of being this way. Keep working with this until all your resentment is gone.

If you still have trouble, forgive as a matter of choice. "I hereby release all resentment for the person. I forgive, just because I say so." You may need to do this over and over.

Make a list all of your resentments and do whatever it takes to release each one.

Action To Take

1. Make a list of every resentment you have.

2. Notice how much you have suffered from your resentments. Are you now willing to be free of the suffering? Are you now willing to be free of your resentment?

3. For each resentment, find the hurt that you are avoiding. What do those circumstances say about you? Then let in the hurt of being this way. Cry the hurt of the circumstances and cry the hurt of what happened.

4. Notice that the person you resent was doing the very best he or she could with the very limited awareness that this person had at the time. Forgive each person for not being wiser and more aware.

5. Work with this chapter until you are totally free of all resentment.

Chapter 17

MAKE PEACE WITH YOUR PARENTS

Most of us have a painful relationship with at least one of our parents. If this is true for you, this is probably where you developed your hurt. That parent would have implied that you were worthless, not good enough or some other form of *not okay*.

As a little child, this would have been extremely painful. To avoid this hurt, and to avoid facing this aspect of you, you put up your walls of protection.

Automatically, you became critical and resentful toward the parent that hurt you. That parent then got upset, put up his or her walls of protection and became even more non-accepting toward you. Then you got hurt even more.

Without knowing, your actions fueled the cycle of conflict. You created more hurt and magnified the feelings of being *not okay*.

Typically, this cycle of conflict continues for a lifetime.

Ending this conflict and healing your relationship with your parents is particularly important. It's important because in order to do this, you must first heal your relationship with you.

Use the following steps to let go of your resistance and to make peace with each of your parents. Work with one parent at a time.

You can also use these steps to heal your relationship with anyone, but work with your parents first.

1. Discover the aspects of you that are being reactivated.

Look at how that person treated you. What did those circumstances say about you? What did that person imply about you in his or her words and actions?

How would you feel if everything that person said about you was the truth – you are so worthless and not good enough that you deserved everything that happened to you?

Obviously, this isn't the truth, but it can certainly be your hurt. Notice if this is a painful thought. If it is, you have found the hurt that runs your life.

Allow yourself to feel the hurt of being this way. Then look at all the evidence to prove that you are this way. This is an aspect of you. Let it in. It's also part of being human.

To the extent that you are able to make peace with this aspect of you, you no longer need to fight and resist this person. You can then heal both your hurt and your relationship.

2. Accept this person the way he or she is.

Notice that this person has a very particular state of mind and way of seeing life. This individual is the way he or she is whether you like it or not.

Let go of your demands for how you believe this person should be and make peace with the way he or she is. You don't have to like it, just surrender to the truth. "I give you full permission to be the way you are, and to be that way forever."

Resisting the way this person is will only make your situation worse.

3. Let go of all your resentment.

Notice that this person is doing the very best he or she can with his or her very limited awareness. Be willing to feel your hurt and forgive the person for not being wiser and more aware.

Use the preceding chapter to be free of any resentment you may have. Work with this until all your resentment is gone.

4. Find your role in the conflict.

Both of you are needed to create and maintain the cycle of conflict. Both of you are 100 percent responsible for the loss of love in your relationship. Find your 100 percent.

Notice how non-accepting, critical and resentful you have been. Notice how you have hurt this person and caused this person to put up his or her walls of protection against you. See how your actions have resulted in the loss of love in your relationship.

This person is also 100 percent responsible, but as long as you blame him or her, you give that person all your power. Once you discover your role in the problem, you can do something about it. You then get your power back.

5. See that you are just like this person.

Any characteristic that you resist in another person is an aspect of you that you resist in yourself. You may not act the person, but characteristic is still in you.

How would you feel, if it were true, that you are just like this person?

If this is an uncomfortable thought, or if you deny that this is true, you have just found another issue. Work with this until you can see that no matter how much may hate it, this is an aspect of you.

Once you discover that you are just like this person, your resistance disappears and gets replaced with compassion.

Until you see that you are just like this person, you will continue to resist and your relationship will continue to suffer.

6. Communicate your hurt and express your love.

After you make peace with the way someone is, the next step is to get with that individual and clean up your relationship. Do this in person, by telephone or by letter.

Tell the person that your relationship is important and that you want to restore the love. Accept responsibility for the conflict and ask to be forgiven. Make sure the person feels loved, accepted and appreciated.

The purpose of this conversation is to restore the love, remove the distance and to shift the way that the two of you interact with each other. Do whatever you can to make this happen.

For more information on healing relationships,

HAVE YOU SUFFERED ENOUGH?

read my book, *How To Heal A Painful Relationship*.

As you heal your relationships, you gain more peace of mind and you become more effective in life.

Action To Take

1. Use the steps in this chapter to make peace with your parents. This is important because in order to do this, you have to heal your hurt.

2. Find the aspects of you that your parents reactivate, and allow yourself to feel the hurt of being this way.

3. Notice that your parents did the best they could with their limited awareness. Accept them for being the way they are, and forgive them for not being wiser and more aware.

4. Tell your parents that you want to heal your relationship. Take 100 percent responsibility for the conflict and ask them to forgive you. Make sure they feel loved, accepted and appreciated.

5. Use this chapter to make peace with anyone that you are resisting.

Chapter 18

ALLOW YOURSELF TO BE HUMAN

Do you remember the example of the little girl? If you were to see the little girl, would you see her as stupid or would you see her as precious? You would see her as precious, of course.

Virtually anyone can see her as precious, but do you think the little girl can? No. The moment she bought the notion that she was stupid, she lost the experience of her preciousness. She didn't lose her preciousness. She just lost the experience of it.

The moment this happened, it was as though she lost her soul. She will then spend the entire rest of her life desperately trying to get it back.

Unfortunately, she will think that the key to getting it back is to somehow become smart. She will then spend enormous amounts of time and energy trying to be smart, but no matter what she does, it will never be enough.

It will never be enough because what she is seeking isn't outside of her. It's inside, and it has never gone anywhere. She just lost the experience of it.

The same thing has happened to you, to me and to everyone else on the planet.

As a little child, you got hurt and bought the notion that you weren't okay. Instantly, you lost the experience of who you are. You are just as precious as the little girl, but you lost your ability to see it.

From that moment on, you'll spend the rest of your life trying to restore the essence of you. You will do everything you can to become worthy, good enough, a success and so on. But no matter what you do, it will never be enough.

Now there is something you can do to get back some of what you have been seeking. There is an exercise that can allow you to rediscover your preciousness.

To get the best results, have someone walk you through the steps or use a tape recorder and play them back. This exercise is a very important part of the healing process. Make sure you take the time to do it.

- Get into a comfortable position and close your eyes.

- Then take a deep breath and allow yourself to relax.

- Now go back in time and see yourself as a little child. See yourself with all the aspects that you have been resisting.

- Take a good look at this child. Isn't this child precious? Isn't this child absolutely wonderful, adorable and lovable, just the way he or she is?

- Isn't this true no matter what aspects are present?

- Now take a look at this preciousness. Notice that this preciousness is the very essence of who you are. It hasn't gone anywhere. You just lost the experience of it.

- Let this in.

- Now bring in the grown child and see this same preciousness.

- Look under the hurt and see your love, and in this love, see your preciousness. It's certainly there. It's the very essence of you.

- Now get with the little child and tell the child how sorry you are for having been so judgmental and critical of him or her. You didn't let the child be human.

- Tell the child how sorry you are for demanding and expecting so much.

- Then ask the child if he or she will please forgive you. Be still and listen to whatever the child has to say.

- Now have a conversation with the child. Make sure both of you say whatever the two of you need to say in order to heal your relationship, and to fall back in love with each other. Take your time.

- When you are finished, give each other a big hug. Then go to another significant age in your life and do the exercise again.

- Do this exercise at every significant age, including you as an adult.

- Then, when you are finished, open your eyes.

Something very special happens when you make peace with yourself. You become more at peace with life.

Own your greatness.

To fully experience who you are and to feel really good about yourself, you need to own every aspect of you. This includes not only the aspects you consider negative, but also the ones you consider positive.

So far, we have only been looking at the negative aspects. Now it's time to own the positive ones.

ALLOW YOURSELF TO BE HUMAN

Often, this is more difficult than owning the negative ones.

The first step in owning your positive aspects is to discover what they are.

Make a list of everything you like about yourself. List all your talents, your abilities and your accomplishments. List everything about you that you are proud of.

Making this list will have you look at yourself in a very different way.

When you finish, read the list to a friend. Brag about yourself. Be proud and read the list boldly. Don't hold back. This may be embarrassing, but telling someone about your positive aspects is the best way to own them.

This exercise is important because if you can't talk about your positive aspects, you won't be able to own them; and if you can't own them, you won't be able to express them.

Consider doing this exercise with several people. Keep expressing your greatness until you realize that this is also an aspect of you.

Then ask several of your friends to list all the things that they admire and respect about you. What do they like about you? What are your gifts, your talents and abilities? What are the aspects of you that make you special?

Listen to what your friends have to say and notice that everything they say about you is the truth. These are aspects of you. You may have to stretch to let this in, but it will be worth the effort.

The more you let in your greatness, the more you will be able to express it in your life.

Allow yourself to be human.

We have been taught that in order to be loved, we have to be worthy, successful or good enough. This is what we have been taught, but it's totally opposite of the truth.

You never love someone because the person is worthy, successful or good enough. You may respect the person but you won't love the person. That person certainly won't melt your heart.

You get your heart melted when someone

allows him or herself to be human, when someone sheds a tear or is willing to be vulnerable. This is what melts your heart.

In one of our workshops, people discover this in a profound way. As we watch people own the aspects that they have been running from, two things happen.

First, you see very clearly that the hurt has nothing to do with the truth. You wonder how the person came up with his or her issue. "Worthless, that's nonsense." "Not good enough? Where did you come up with that?"

Second, you fall madly in love with the person. As the person owns his or her hurt, that person becomes very human and melts your heart. You feel safe. You feel loved and you become much more able to be yourself.

The same thing happens when you own your worthlessness. Your ego stands aside. You become very human and you create the experience of love.

It may seem uncomfortable to be human, but this is the key to having more love than you have ever had in your life. It's also the key to having your dreams come true.

As you allow yourself to be human, you tap into a power much greater than you. You become an expression of love. You light up the world and life works for you instead of against you.

Life is so much easier when you allow yourself to be human.

ALLOW YOURSELF TO BE HUMAN

Action To Take

1. Use the inner child exercise to heal your relationship with yourself. Do this exercise at each age that has been significant in your life. This exercise is very important.

2. Make a list of everything that you like about yourself. List your talents, your abilities and your accomplishments. List everything about yourself that you are proud of. Then read the list to a friend. Use this exercise to own your greatness.

3. Then contact several of your friends and have them tell you all the positive qualities that they see in you. Notice that everything they say about you is the truth. Let it in.

4. Allow yourself to be human. Own both the positive and negative aspects of you. This is the key to creating love and having life work for you instead of against you.

Chapter 19

THE OPPORTUNITY IS YOURS

When you were little, you were pure love. You were happy, alive and free. You were fearless, creative and could flow with almost anything. Life was an exciting adventure.

Then you got hurt and started closing down. You bought the notion that you weren't okay and that you needed to be different than you were. Instantly, you lost your ability to be human.

You then spent the rest of your life avoiding this hurt, trying to become a certain way. In the process, you pushed away love and created your own fear, upset and suffering.

Now you have an opportunity to reverse the process. You can heal your hurt and set yourself free inside. As you do this, you restore the love that you are. You become more human and more able to create a life that works.

To heal your hurt, you need to remove the resistance that creates it. You need to discover and make peace with the aspects of you that you've been resisting.

Use this book to make peace with as many aspects of you as you can. Then go through life looking for more. Look for upsets and look for any area of your life where you can't flow.

Whenever you can't flow with something, some hurt in you is being reactivated. To find what the hurt is, ask yourself, "What do those circumstances say about me?"

Find the aspects of you that you've been resisting and make peace with them. The more you do this, the more you are able to flow with life and the more effective you become.

At first, you will be working with the most obvious hurt. Then you will discover new hurt and deeper levels of old hurt.

As time goes on, the upsets in your life become

fewer and fewer. Life becomes more enjoyable and more of your dreams come true.

The process for setting yourself free inside is relatively simple, but it doesn't happen by itself. You have to take action. Make healing your hurt a top priority. It's one of the most important things you can ever do.

Life is to short too have it be anything less than a joy.

Thank you and
I love you.

Bill Ferguson

This is a book you will want to read over and over again. Every time you read it, you will heal more of your hurt, and you will become more effective in your life.

If you want to learn more about how to be free inside and how to have your life work, attend our programs, read our books and listen to our audio cassettes and CDs.

THE OPPORTUNITY IS YOURS

If you want to have a telephone consulting session with me or a member of my staff, call us at (713) 520-5370.

You can also find us on the Internet at:

www.billferguson.com
www.effectiveliving.com
www.divorceasfriends.com

BOOKS, TAPES & CDs

HAVE YOU SUFFERED ENOUGH?

Be Free Of The Hidden Core Issues That Destroy Love And Sabotage Your Life.

This book is also available on audio cassettes & CDs.

Paperback, 144 pages

Ultimately, all of our suffering and all of our self-sabotaging behavior are the result of hidden core issues from the past. These issues are created by the automatic avoidance of a very specific hurt. When these issues get triggered, they produce a state of fear and upset that destroys love and forces us to interact in a way that sabotages our lives. Finding and healing this hurt is one of the most important things you can ever do. This book will show you how.

ISBN 1-878410-28-8	Paperback	$15
ISBN 1-878410-32-6	Two Audio Cassettes	$18
ISBN 1-878410-33-4	Two CDs	$22

HOW TO HEAL A PAINFUL RELATIONSHIP

And If Necessary, How To Part As Friends

This book is also available on audio cassettes & CDs.

Paperback, 156 pages

In this unique book, Bill Ferguson shows, step-by-step, how to remove conflict and restore love in any relationship. You will learn what creates love and what destroys it. You will discover how to end the cycle of conflict, heal hurt, release resentment and restore your peace of mind. Bill's experience as a former divorce attorney provides rare insight into the nature of relationships. You will discover something about yourself and your relationships that will change your life forever.

ISBN 1-878410-25-3	Paperback	$12
ISBN 1-878410-26-1	Two Audio Cassettes	$16
ISBN 1-878410-31-8	Two CDs	$25

MIRACLES ARE GUARANTEED

A Step-By-Step Guide To Restoring Love, Being Free And Creating A Life That Works.

Paperback, 160 pages

This book shows, step-by-step, how to have love in every aspect of life. You will learn how to heal your hurt and set yourself free inside. You will learn how to clean up your life and be free of upset and stress. You will discover how to take charge of your life, find your life purpose and experience your spirituality. This profound yet simple book covers all the steps to having life work.

ISBN 1-878410-20-2   Paperback $11

BOOKS, TAPES & CDs

HOW TO DIVORCE AS FRIENDS

And Maybe Save Your Marriage

Four audio cassettes or two CDs

These tapes and CDs show, step-by-step, how to end conflict and restore cooperation in even the most difficult relationships. You will learn how to heal your hurt, be free of resentment and resolve issues quickly. You will learn how to heal your relationship one human being to another.

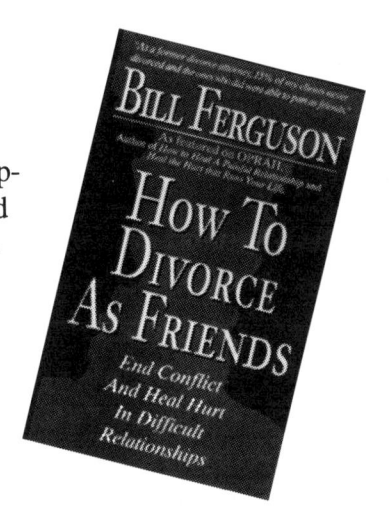

Tape 1 - End The Cycle Of Conflict. - Learn how to end conflict, let go and restore your peace of mind.

Tape 2 - Heal Your Hurt. - Find and heal the inner issues that create your pain and sabotage your relationship.

Tape 3 - Clean Up Your Relationship. - Learn how to communicate and how to be free of guilt, anger, resentment and blaming.

Tape 4 - Resolve Issues Peacefully. - Learn how to resolve your issues without conflict.

ISBN 1-878410-24-5 Four Audio Cassettes...........................$25
ISBN 1-878410-29-6 Two CDs..$25

BOOKS, TAPES & CDs

Set yourself free & enjoy your life

This album includes each of the following 8 audio cassettes for only $65.

Individual cassettes are available for $10.

These audio cassettes show, step-by-step, how to create a life that works.

ISBN 1-878410-01-6 $65

How To Love Yourself
- Be free of self-invalidation.
- Release the issues that run your life.
- Love yourself just the way you are.

ISBN 1-878410-02-4 $10

How To Have Love In Your Life
- Discover what creates love.
- Learn how to communicate effectively.
- Have love in all your relationships.

ISBN 1-878410-03-2 $10

BOOKS, TAPES & CDs

How To Be Free Of Guilt And Resentments
- Be free of all anger, resentment and guilt.
- Restore your inner peace.
- Have difficult relationships work.

ISBN 1-878410-04-0 $10

How To Be Free Of Upset and Stress
- Be at peace in any situation.
- Release the mechanisms that keep you upset.
- Restore your piece of mind.

ISBN 1-878410-05-9 $10

How To Create Prosperity
- Release the mechanism that creates lack and financial stress.
- Remove your blocks to prosperity.
- Learn how to create abundance.

ISBN 1-878410-06-7 $10

How To Create A Life That Works
- Discover how you create your own unworkability.
- Be free of the hidden actions that sabotage you.
- Learn how to clean up your life.

ISBN 1-878410-07-5 $10

BOOKS, TAPES & CDs

How To Find Your Purpose
- Earn a living doing what you love.
- Have your life make a difference.
- Discover your life purpose.

ISBN 1-878410-08-3 $10

How To Experience Your Spirituality
- Connect with your life force.
- Experience being one with God.
- Discover the Light.

ISBN 1-878410-09-1 $10

SPIRITUALITY: TEACHINGS FROM A WORLD BEYOND

Two audio cassettes

Several years ago, some profound teachings were received through a form of meditation. Since then, thousands of people have had their lives deeply altered. Through these teachings, you will discover the essence of spirituality. You will experience a oneness with God and will discover a truth that can profoundly alter your life.

ISBN 1-878410-11-3 $16

TO ORDER BOOKS, TAPES & CDs

Item		Price	Qty	Amount
Have You Suffered Enough?	Paperback	$15		
	2 Audio Tapes	$18		
	2 CDs	$22		
How to Heal A Painful Relationship	Paperback	$12		
	2 Audio Tapes	$16		
	2 CDs	$22		
Miracles Are Guaranteed	Paperback	$11		
How To Divorce As Friends	4 Audio Tapes	$25		
	2 CDs	$25		
Set Yourself Free This album includes each of the following 8 audio tapes		$65		
• How To Love Yourself	Audio Tape	$10		
• How To Have Love In Your Life	Audio Tape	$10		
• How To Be Free Of Guilt And Resentment	Audio Tape	$10		
• How To Be Free Of Upset And Stress	Audio Tape	$10		
• How To Create Prosperity	Audio Tape	$10		
• How To Create A Life That Works	Audio Tape	$10		
• How To Find Your Purpose	Audio Tape	$10		
• How To Experience Your Spirituality	Audio Tape	$10		
Spirituality: Teachings	2 Audio Tapes	$16		
	Subtotal			
	Texas residents add 8% sales tax			
Shipping and handling: Add 10% of Subtotal $4 minimum, $10 maximum				
	Total			

Name (Please print) _____

Address _____

City _____

State _____ Zip _____

Telephone Day ( ) _____ Evening ( ) _____

For credit card orders:

Card No. _____ Total $ _____

Exp. Date _____ Signature _____

Send your order along with your check or money order to:
Return to the Heart, P.O. Box 541813, Houston, Texas 77254

For Telephone orders, call (713) 520-5370
www.billferguson.com • www.effectiveliving.com
www.divorceasfriends.com

If you want to have a telephone consultation with Bill Ferguson or a member of his staff, call us at (713) 520-5370.

You can find us on the internet at
www.billferguson.com
www.effectiveliving.com
www.divorceasfriends.com